Original title:
Rosy Reflections

Copyright © 2025 Creative Arts Management OÜ
All rights reserved.

Author: Dean Whitmore
ISBN HARDBACK: 978-1-80566-656-1
ISBN PAPERBACK: 978-1-80566-941-8

Embracing the Sunset

The sun wears a crown of bright hues,
As it dances, skimming through pinks and blues.
I chase the shadows, but they are sly,
They wink and tease as they wave goodbye.

Kites swoop low, flirting with my hat,
While squirrels debate which tree is where it's at.
Laughter echoes off the fading light,
As I trip on air, oh what a sight!

Petal-Laden Whispers

A flower sneezes, pollen flies,
The bees all giggle and roll their eyes.
Petals gossip, blushing bright red,
About the shy stems, who'd rather play dead.

Gardener grumbles, spills soil galore,
While the tulips snicker, begging for more.
Nature's buffet on a picnic spread,
Who knew daisies could end up in bed?

The Garden's Embrace

A hedgehog pranced, in a leafy groove,
While daisies attempted a cartwheel move.
The moon chuckled, peeking through trees,
As frogs serenaded, hoping for a breeze.

Butterflies danced, in dazzling pairs,
Chasing each other without any cares.
Each flower blushing, trying to impress,
While bumblebees buzzed in a fancy dress.

Elysian Petals

In a realm where clovers wear silly hats,
And daisies gossip about lazy cats.
The sun tickles blooms with golden rays,
As I join in their whimsical, wild plays.

The earth rolls its eyes, has seen it all,
While tulips wait for my next stumble and fall.
Yet in this chuckle-filled, blooming spree,
Even the weeds are laughing at me!

Blossoms Between Us

In a garden filled with laughter,
Petals dance, pausing in mirth.
Bees buzz around in silly chatter,
While we joke about our worth.

Sunflowers bow with a grin,
Tulips giggle in the sun.
Daisies tease the wild wind,
Planting smiles, just for fun.

The Reflective Bloom

In the pond, a frog does leap,
Its reflection looks quite absurd.
Winking, it makes the lily weep,
And the goldfish stares, undeterred.

Butterflies wear silly hats,
Strutting like they own the scene.
With every flap, they drop their snacks,
Creating chaos, quite routine.

Moments on the Breeze

A dandelion takes a trip,
Blowing wishes into the air.
It makes a jump, does a flip,
Leaves my thoughts floating with flair.

A squirrel joins in on the fun,
Chasing its tail in circles tight.
It stops to bask beneath the sun,
In a game of tag with delight.

Tides of Delicate Light

Sunset spills its colors wide,
Tickling trees with golden beams.
Laughter rides the gentle tide,
As crickets chirp their nightly themes.

Fireflies waltz in playful flight,
Glowing fools in the darkened lane.
A moonbeam sparkles with delight,
Whispering jokes that feel insane.

Harmony in Pink

In a world so bright, we wear shades,
Giggles abound in pastel parades.
Candy clouds float over the town,
Where laughter flows like a pink gown.

Tiny feet dance on sugary grounds,
Chasing dreams with silly sounds.
Butterflies tickle with every cheer,
Creating moments we hold dear.

Vivid Fragments of Time

Snapshots of laughter in sticky frames,
We scribble our joys, giving them names.
Jellybean skies and marshmallow suns,
In this crazy circus, everyone runs.

Tickled by time in this whimsical place,
A muddle of smiles on each painted face.
We trip on our giggles, fall in delight,
In a kaleidoscope world, everything's right.

Veils of the Past

Old photos hiding in dusty corners,
Whispering secrets like cheeky sorners.
Grandma's wiggle and grandpa's dance,
Replaying history with a silly glance.

Cuckoo clocks giggle, and time skews,
Wearing mismatched socks with brightly hues.
We blend all the past with a fond jest,
In this gallery of memories, we're all blessed.

Scented Time Capsules

A jar full of laughter, tucked away tight,
Sprinkled with giggles that feel just right.
Bubblegum wisdom from years gone by,
Frothy dreams drifting like cotton candy sky.

With every pop, a tickle of cheer,
Time capsules burst, and memories reappear.
Silly smells of crayons and cake,
Remind us of joy in every mistake.

Sunset Whispers

The sun dips low, a winking eye,
The clouds parade, like puffs up high.
Colors are spilling, a giggling delight,
Nature's canvas glows in the twilight.

Crickets join in, they chirp a tune,
As shadows play, beneath the moon.
A sly raccoon scuttles, oh what a sight,
Stealing the snacks from the picnic tonight.

Garden of Hushed Secrets

In a garden where whispers like petals fall,
Gnomes are gossiping, oh they're having a ball!
Butterflies flutter, with scandalous flair,
While daisies gossip with a breeze in their hair.

The tomatoes are blushing, ripe and so red,
Even the weeds seem to giggle instead.
"Who'll pick the veggies?" the pumpkins debate,
They burst into laughter, can't stand the wait.

Velvet Glimmers

Under velvet skies, the stars play tricks,
Constellations twinkle, with laughter they mix.
The moon drops a wink, oh what a tease,
While dark clouds giggle, sailing with ease.

A comet whizzes by, what a wild race,
Sending sparkling puffs, all over the place.
The night holds secrets, wrapped up in fun,
As dreams burst forth, like bubbles undone.

Petals in the Wind

Petals tumble down, a floral ballet,
They swirl and they twirl, in a breezy display.
Bees buzz in sync, with their tiny little tunes,
As blossoms chuckle, under sunny afternoons.

A gust takes a rose for a wild ride,
Spinning and flipping, oh how it's styled!
Laughter of flowers, a fragrant delight,
Each petal a giggle, painting the night.

Fragments of a Dream

In my sleep, I chase a cat,
With a monocle and a top hat.
He offers tea, but spills it all,
We laugh and bounce like a rubber ball.

The ceiling dances with bright spots,
While the walls wear polka-dots.
A chocolate fountain springs to life,
Turns my slippers into buttered knife.

Through laughter's lens, dreams unfold,
A circus of antics, bright and bold.
Jellybeans rain from the skies,
With each one comes a funny surprise.

Awake, I find it all a joke,
A merry tale, all smoke and poke.
Yet in my heart, the joy's still gleams,
In silly twists of sweetened dreams.

Shades of Tenderness

A kitten playing with a bell,
It strikes a note, oh what the swell!
It sings a tune, but not so good,
Like a choir of squirrels, misunderstood.

Underneath the gnarled old tree,
A compact clown is tickling me.
He turns to me with colored face,
And dances like he's won a race.

Balloons in hand, they twist and twirl,
A salad of colors, watch them swirl.
With every pop, a giggle escapes,
Like silly stories of cartoon shapes.

Tender moments bubble and burst,
With funny antics, I feel immersed.
In laughter's glow, we gently share,
These shades of joy, beyond compare.

The Language of Blush

A beetroot wearing a silly grin,
Tries to tell jokes, it's a comedic win.
Each laugh causes it to turn bright,
As it whispers puns tucked in the night.

With strawberries that dance in a bowl,
They tango lightly, each takes a stroll.
Berry giggles float in the air,
Creating blush from all the flare.

A muffin wearing a party hat,
Decides to compete with a talking cat.
They tumble about, a delightful sight,
In this world of sweetness, pure delight.

And here we sit, in giggles abound,
With berry blush, we spin around.
In silly moments, we find our way,
Laughing until the end of day.

Delicate Mirrors

In mirrors, reflections hug and sway,
They twist and shout, in playful array.
With every glance, a silly mime,
Turns my frown into a peek-a-boo rhyme.

The knick-knack shelf sings a tune,
Through tiny spoons that start to croon.
With every glance, the laughter starts,
As my socks join in with happy hearts.

Charming cups with winking eyes,
Whisper secrets, oh, what a surprise.
One told me of a dancing cake,
That performs pirouettes just for fate.

Delicate mirrors and jolly prank,
Reflecting moods that rise and clank.
In this realm, where giggles shine,
Every glance ignites the divine.

Blossom Dances

In gardens green, the flowers sway,
Bees buzzing loud, they sing and play.
Petals twirl in a silly show,
A clumsy dance, as breezes blow.

Skirts of daisies lift and twine,
Butterflies sip on sweet sunshine.
Tulips giggle, paint the ground,
Nature's laugh, a joyful sound.

Wiggly roots beneath the ground,
Whisper tales of laughter found.
Each bloom a jester, chasing fear,
Tickling noses, bringing cheer.

In the garden, jokes are told,
Sunlight sparkles, bright and bold.
A blossom's bounce, a petal's flight,
A party blooms in pure delight.

The Tinge of First Love

In springtime air, hearts flutter high,
With blushes bright and silly sighs.
Two shy smiles peek from behind the trees,
Like tangled vines in a playful breeze.

A secret note with a squiggly heart,
Ink spills like laughter; that's just the start.
Crushes giggle with a nervous glance,
Each little moment, a wobbly dance.

Ice cream drips while fingers meet,
Sticky sweet on tangled feet.
Whispers soft, they float like dreams,
The world spins on, or so it seems.

Underneath the twinkling stars,
The moonlight jokes, the night is ours.
Two hearts stumble, then take the leap,
In the hallowed air, memories keep.

Reflections in Bloom

A pond of giggles, splashes clear,
Where frogs croak jokes we hold dear.
Reeds stand tall with a playful stance,
Nature's mirror reflects the dance.

Ducks waddle by in quacking glee,
As petals mix in fancy spree.
Their colorful hats, a fashion blunder,
A game of hide and seek, in wonder.

Ripples ripple, a ticklish game,
As sunlight dapples, none the same.
A heron struts, a feathery clown,
In a watery world, never a frown.

Bubbles rise with a popping laugh,
Reflections share their silly craft.
Each little splash a giggly tune,
Nature hums beneath the moon.

Painted Moments

With a brush made of sunlight bright,
We splash on colors, pure delight.
Canvases dance, with swirls of fun,
Joyful hues, as day is done.

Mismatched socks and plaid shirts collide,
Artistic flair we cannot hide.
Each stroke tells tales of laughter shared,
In quirky shades, none are scared.

Brushes mingle in a clumsy way,
Making rainbows, come what may.
Splotches everywhere, a merry mess,
Life's a canvas, we must confess.

As the sunset paints the sky,
We tip our hats to clouds up high.
In painted moments, let's be free,
Creating art, just you and me.

Glittering Petals

Petals dance in the breeze,
Tickling noses, oh what a tease!
They tumble down with a flick and spin,
Who knew flowers could cause such a grin?

In gardens where giggles float around,
Silly squirrels chase crickets they found.
Butterflies whisper, they'll never arrive,
With alligator shoes, they surely strive!

A ladybug struts, wearing a hat,
While a bumbling bee hugs a well-fed rat.
The flowers all chuckle, they quietly say,
"Check out that bird! What a wobbly display!"

In the cool shade with laughter and cheer,
Nature's a circus, always near.
So let's skip and hop, let joy unfurl,
In this garden of giggles, come give it a whirl!

The Soft Glow of Yesterday

In the twilight, the sun waves goodbye,
As moths in tuxedos begin to fly.
They bump and they fumble, with glittery bling,
Turning the night into a dance to swing!

Fireflies giggle, winking with glee,
"Catch us if you can!" says one lively bee.
They twirl round the daisies with a daring spin,
While frogs in the pond burst into a grin.

The moon joins the laughter, wearing a crown,
Casting its light on the breeze of the town.
The night, with its quirks, begins to parade,
As playful shadows join in the charade.

So now let the laughter twinkle and spin,
In the soft glow where all the fun begins.
With a wink and a chuckle, we drift into play,
While yesterday's dreams dance gently away.

Dappled Reflections

In puddles of joy, laughter reflects,
With giggles of daisies, springtime connects.
The frogs leap high, in their stylish hats,
Hopping alongside the chirping chitchats.

Dappled light feasts on the silly scene,
As the squirrels are plotting, oh what a routine!
With acorns in tow, they're planning mischief,
While bumblebees buzz, sharing a riff.

Sunbeams poke through, with a playful wink,
As turtles flip coins near the river's brink.
Each ripple a chuckle, each wave a cheer,
Nature's surprise is undeniably clear!

So let's skip through the laughter, let worries be few,
In the dappled reflections, a colorful hue.
With friends made of petals, we twirl and we prance,
In this delightful garden, come join the dance!

Where Petals Fall

Where petals tumble and giggles ignite,
Wobbly bees buzz on such a fine night.
With butterflies flapping in mismatched shoes,
They join the flower dance with some joyful news!

A dandelion sings, with a voice quite absurd,
"Why do you flutter, oh silly old bird?"
While ladybugs laugh in their polka dot dress,
Creating a ruckus, oh what a mess!

The moonlight playfully dances on grass,
As clouds whisper rumors that make the stars laugh.
In a world of joy, the night wears a smile,
Every giggle and chuckle echoes for miles.

So wherever the petals decide to land,
Let cheer sprinkle softly upon the land.
Gather around, let the antics begin,
In this fun-filled adventure, together we'll win!

Illusions of Warmth

In a garden where laughter grows,
The sun tickles toes, the wind throws.
A fan dances with petals in flight,
Who knew breezes could feel so light?

Butterflies gossip, they flutter and flit,
While bees wear sunglasses, they won't commit.
A picnic blanket, a cake that won't stay,
Who knew snacks could dance and sway?

The sun sets low, a vibrant burst,
But really, it's just a candy's first thirst.
Ice cream cones melt in the warm embrace,
As kids chase dreams, they can't keep pace.

In this realm of giggles, nothing is tough,
With hugs made of giggles, life's silly enough.

Woven Petals

A tapestry made of petals so bright,
With daisies gossiping under the night.
Tulips wear hats, very dapper indeed,
It's a floral party, watch out for the seed!

The roses compete for the best dance moves,
While sunflowers laugh, losing all grooves.
Petals are weaving, a colorful mess,
A vine starts to twirl; I must confess!

A bee tells a joke that leaves all in stitches,
While ladybugs glide over flowerbed ditches.
In this giggle garden, all worries drop,
When petals are dancing, the fun won't stop!

With blooms as our buddies, we can't fall flat,
In this swirling circus, let's tip our hat!

Crimson Echoes

In a field where echoes of laughter arise,
Crimson blooms sparkle, like joyful eyes.
A squirrel dons shades, thinks he's so cool,
While daisies play hopscotch, breaking the rule.

The wind carries secrets, whispers so sweet,
With petals that giggle, skipping on feet.
A red balloon tries to take flight and fails,
But laughter takes shape on the butterfly trails.

Poppies ballroom dance under dazzling light,
Their swirls and twirls are quite a sight.
Rainbow-colored bees join in the cheer,
It's hard not to smile when joy's so near.

In this mischievous garden, let worries flee,
With crimson echoes, we'll dance 'til we're free!

Petals Beneath the Surface

Beneath the leaves, where quirks often sleep,
Petals plot mischief, promises to keep.
A weed thinks it's fancy with a new hat,
While snails in tuxedos respond to that!

Sunlight makes shadows that wiggle and laugh,
As bunnies skip by, they craft their own path.
A hidden treasure, a lost shoe revealed,
The garden of giggles is forever concealed.

A gopher performs with his fancy new grin,
As flowers keep time with the dance of the wind.
Petals exchange rumors, they giggle in glee,
Who knew flowers had such a wild spree?

Underneath the surface, laughter takes root,
Whispers of petals lead to a hoot!

Whispers of the Heart

A little birdie told me so,
You're the star of the show,
With a wink and a playful grin,
Life feels like it's about to begin.

You wear mismatched socks today,
In a most charming way,
Your laughter's a bubbling brook,
Come closer, have a look!

The cake fell but who cares,
Let's dance without any fears,
With sprinkles in our hair,
Life's a silly affair!

So spin around, twist and shout,
Join the fun without a doubt,
Tomorrow might be a mess,
But today, let's wear our best!

Echoes of Soft Light

In the glow of the midnight lamp,
You tell tales and go on a ramp,
With giggles that sparkle and shine,
Your quirky jokes make everything fine.

The cat wears a hat, isn't that grand?
Next to the dog, who can barely stand,
They prance like they own the street,
What a delightful, funny feat!

Jelly beans rain down from above,
It's a sticky, sweet kind of love,
Dance with shadows, just let go,
In this light, we steal the show!

So here we are with our gleeful strife,
Turning each moment into life,
Join the wild, ridiculous ride,
With laughter as our joyful guide!

Dance of the Blossoms

Petals twirl and whirl around,
In a dainty, giggly sound,
Silly bees buzz to a tune,
Underneath a playful moon.

A snail in boots moves with flair,
Through the garden, unaware,
While daisies whisper sweet dreams,
In patches of sunlit beams.

Butterflies join the frolicsome crew,
Fluttering without a clue,
Chasing shadows with delight,
Oh, what a whimsical sight!

So let's join their merry game,
Adding joy to life's sweet frame,
In every twirl and every spin,
We find the laughter deep within!

Dreams in Full Bloom

In a garden where giggles grow,
Every flower has its glow,
They nod and chuckle at the sun,
Together, we all have fun.

On a swing made of daffodils,
We soar over laughter-filled hills,
And if we tumble, let's not cry,
We'll just bounce and touch the sky!

With jelly fish doing the cha-cha,
And turtles sipping on soda,
We'll blend the odd with the sweet,
In this jovial world, life's a treat!

So grab a friend and join the spree,
Dance like everyone's a bee,
In dreams where humor blooms loud,
Let our laughter make us proud!

Hues of Hope

In a garden of giggles and dreams,
A flower's blush bursts at the seams.
Bumblebees waltz in the bright sun,
Chasing each other, just having fun.

Petals parade in a clumsy sway,
Tickling noses, come what may.
Frogs croak jokes from the lily pads,
While sunflowers giggle, oh, aren't they mad?

Bright marigolds joke with the thyme,
Saying, "We'll bloom just one more time!"
In the midst of laughter and light,
Who wouldn't dance in sheer delight?

So let us dance, let us play,
In hues of humor, greet the day!
Forget the frowns, let joy unfold,
With a splash of colors, be bold!

A Canvas of Soft Light

Brushstrokes of laughter, light so sweet,
As colors twirl, twinkling feet.
Dandelions join in the cheer,
Spinning their tales, sipping clear beer.

Clouds painted pink with a dash of gold,
Whispering secrets of stories bold.
Chasing butterflies with silly grace,
Even the sun wears a playful face.

The canvas stretches, unfolding wide,
A whimsical world where dreams abide.
Brushes tickle, with every stroke,
In this land, all worries choke.

So let's splash joy, wild and free,
Creating a masterpiece, you and me!
With laughter and light, let's ignite,
This canvas of soft, delightful sight!

A Symphony of Roses

A symphony blooms in the bright, warm air,
With note-laden petals, beauty to share.
Roses waltz with the daffodils near,
Strumming soft tunes that tickle the ear.

In the midst of giggles, a bumblebee's tune,
Buzzing about like a cheeky cartoon.
With purple pansies cracking jokes,
While petunias blush at the silly folks.

A rose dips low for a quick, bold spin,
While daisies cheer, "Let the fun begin!"
Zinnias giggle, it's a wild sight,
In this musical garden, hearts feel light.

So let the blossoms fill the air,
With melodies bright, without a care.
In this garden where laughter grows,
Join the symphony of bright, bold prose!

Gentle Mornings

Gentle mornings, a whimsical sight,
As sunbeams dance, oh what delight!
Roosters crow with a rhythmic beat,
While sleepy heads rise, dragging their feet.

Coffee breezes with a cheeky grin,
Whispers of warmth, let the day begin.
Socks mismatched hop on the floor,
As knickers giggle, wanting more.

Eggs flip with flair, toast jumps high,
While butter spreads, oh me, oh my!
Sunshine tickles the waking world,
As breakfast banter lazily twirled.

So savor the chuckles of morning bliss,
In a kaleidoscope of laughter's kiss.
Each new day, a delightful quest,
With gentle beginnings, we're truly blessed!

Blush of Dawn

The sun peeks in with a grin,
Tickling the curtains, let the fun begin.
Coffee spills, oh what a sight,
Looks like I've won the morning fight!

Pancakes flip like they have a mind,
Syrup rivers, sweetness unconfined.
Butter melts like dreams on toast,
I toast my breakfast, it's the best host!

A cat leaps and lands with flair,
Knocks my plans out of the air.
Chasing shadows, a furry mess,
Who knew mornings could be such a stress?

But laughter bubbles, it's time to jest,
Today's adventure awaits the best.
With smiles wide, let's raise a cheer,
For every blush that brings us near.

Fragrant Echoes

Flowers dance in the gentle breeze,
Whisper secrets, oh you tease.
A daisy winks, a rose gives chase,
In this garden, we find our place.

Buzzing bees on a mission so grand,
Coffee cups stuck in the sand.
"Dare you to taste the pollen divine!"
Life's simple joys in every line.

Butterflies flitter like tiny clowns,
Wearing colors that dazzle the towns.
They tease the flowers, full of glee,
While ants march on, "You'll never catch me!"

The sun sets low, wearing a smile,
Filling our hearts, rimming the aisle.
With fragrant echoes of laughter sweet,
In this garden, life's truly a treat.

Petal-Pink Reverie

In a dream where colors collide,
Petals float down as if they've lied.
Each step leads to a chuckle or two,
In a world where sighing feels brand new.

Silly squirrels in a flower parade,
Wearing hats that a child had made.
Jumping jacks, they frolic with flair,
Branches creak as they dance in the air.

The sky's a canvas, splashed up high,
Cloud shapes dance, oh, how they fly!
"Look!" I shout, "A cat in a hat!"
As giggles swell, I tip my mat.

With petal-pink dreams swirling about,
I shout at the clouds, "Let's party, no doubt!"
In this reverie, joy's the decree,
Let's paint the world with liveliness, whee!

Reflections in Bloom

Mirrors crack with a comic twist,
What stares back? An untouchable list!
A mop of curls like a frizzy beard,
Did they sprout or am I just weird?

Sunflowers giggle, their heads held high,
"Smile!" they say, "You're not that shy!"
A daffodil does a silly dance,
"Come join me, take a chance!"

In fields of laughter, we make a scene,
Nature's antics, a fun routine.
A puddle jumps as I plop right in,
Splashes and giggles, where to begin?

Reflections bloom with every glance,
In this carnival, we'll take a chance.
For every misstep, we just assume,
Life's the stage, we're free to zoom!

Secrets in the Garden

In a garden where gnomes wear hats,
The daisies gossip about the cats.
Rabbits dance with a twist and turn,
While weary bees take their afternoon burn.

The sun slips in, with a clever grin,
Tickling the leaves, where secrets begin.
A sunflower yawns, its petals wide,
Winking at the herbs that stand by side.

A frog in shades sings a tune so loud,
As carrots debate what makes them proud.
Bumblebees buzz with a cheeky jest,
In the garden's heart, we find the best.

So wander through, with a curious glance,
Join the daisies in their merry dance.
For in this patch of green and bloom,
Laughter hides behind each colorful plume.

A Brush with Spring

A squirrel prances with style and flair,
Painting the breeze with a dash of air.
Tulips giggle as they wake from dreams,
While raindrops dance on their vibrant beams.

The robin croons a silly, sweet song,
As petals twirl like they've done nothing wrong.
Dandelions puff up their cheeks with pride,
Sending wishes on the wind to glide.

Butterflies play hopscotch on the breeze,
As the sun tickles the bumblebees.
With such chaos, will winter even dare?
To come back and spoil this springtime affair?

So grab your paints and let's make a scene,
In this canvas where joy reigns supreme.
For laughter blooms in each splash and fling,
When nature's in charge, it's a comical spring.

Luminous Melodies

Fireflies flicker, a concert of light,
Sparkling with giggles, a magical sight.
Crickets play tunes on their tiny guitars,
While the moon lights up the night with its stars.

The chatty owls in their wise old trees,
Share jokes and riddles with the buzzing bees.
A raccoon tap dances on the garden gate,
As night wears on, it's never too late.

With a wink and a puff, the night starts to sing,
Echoing laughter that the stars will bring.
In the darkest moments, find the glow,
Where goofy shadows come out to show.

So dance with the fireflies, let spirits soar,
Join this whimsical choir, forevermore.
For in the luminous night of merry glee,
We find that humor is the best melody.

Cherished Impressions

A butterfly flutters with mismatched shoes,
Leaving behind a trail of colorful news.
The daisies gossip as they brush their hair,
With petals so soft, they float in the air.

A turtle races, but oh, what a sight,
Tripped on its shell in the warm golden light.
While ladybugs giggle, a pretty parade,
Chasing after dreams that are just being made.

Clouds wear their grins like a silly hat,
Casting playful shadows where the toddlers sat.
Each puddle sparkles with a splatter of fun,
Reflecting warm smiles as bright as the sun.

So cherish the moments that tickle your heart,
In this world of laughter, let joy be your art.
For every small giggle is sweet to share,
A memory made, forever laid bare.

Tinted Glimpses

Seeing colors in the brew,
Sipping giggles, oh what a view!
Rainbows dance in coffee cups,
Laughter bubbles, who needs the ups?

Cats in hats purr by the fire,
While silly squirrels fuel their desire.
Sunshine spills on pancake stacks,
Each syrup drop sparks funny laughs.

Jellybeans jump with glee,
Tangoing sweetly, just wait and see.
Chocolate rivers flow with charms,
While we twirl in candy farms.

In dreams, we fly on cookie wings,
Through marshmallow fields where joy sings.
A wacky world where giggles reign,
And sunshine dances through the rain.

Floral Reverberations

Petals whisper secrets shy,
While daisies wink and butterflies fly.
Silly bees hum a disco tune,
As tulips wear their best costume.

Sunflowers sway in a bold ballet,
Chasing rainclouds away all day.
Each bloom is a colorful jester,
In this garden, nature's festival is best, sir!

Daffodils giggle in bright yellow hues,
Talking about gossip and morning dew.
Snapdragons snap with a playful bite,
While daisies tease the sun all night.

A frolicsome meadow filled with cheer,
Where every petal dances near.
Oh, what a laugh, a secret shared,
In floral dreams, none are scared!

Radiant Reminiscence

Memories glance with a cheeky grin,
Tickling thoughts of where we've been.
Flying kites in a breeze so sweet,
Chasing clouds down the sunny street.

Silly socks in mismatched pairs,
Racing down hills without cares.
Rocking chairs whisper past delights,
While shadows dance in glowing lights.

Ice cream drips on little hands,
As laughter echoes in sunlit lands.
Each giggle a spark, a burst of fun,
Like goofy races when the day's done.

Time skips joyfully like a child,
As every memory is brightly wild.
A treasure trove filled with light,
In kaleidoscopes of pure delight.

Shades of Soft Dawn

Morning yawns in hues of peach,
Whispering secrets that sunlight will teach.
Jokes are shared on dew-kissed grass,
While sleepy heads make silly sass.

Breezes tickle as they softly tease,
Waking flowers with a playful breeze.
Roosters crow in eccentric tones,
Making melodies that no one owns.

Pancake towers, syrupy delight,
Giggling as they topple in the light.
Juice splashes like a cheerful fight,
Creating chaos, a pure delight!

As day unfurls its light, we soar,
Wandering through laughter's open door.
In shades of dawn, a fun array,
Bringing silly smiles to start the day.

Sun-Kissed Reflections

In the morning light, I squint my eyes,
A bird swoops low, what a surprise!
It drops a worm right on my face,
I laugh and wipe in the sunny space.

The sunbeams dance on my silly hat,
I trip on my shoes, how about that!
Mirrors shimmer as I prance along,
My reflection sings a funny song.

A butterfly lands on my nose,
And off it flits, oh, how it goes!
I try to catch it, but I stumble back,
Into the garden, on the bright green track.

Laughter echoes through the trees,
As I chase shadows and tease the bees.
Life is a game, so come join the fun,
Under the sun, our antics have begun!

Violet Horizons

At dusk, the sky wears a violet hue,
I spot a squirrel with a berry or two.
It shakes its tail and scurries away,
Leaving me laughing at the end of the day.

The clouds like cotton candy drift high,
I wonder if pigeons can learn to fly by.
My neighbor's cat is eyeing me close,
With a look that says, "I've seen the most!"

I blow bubbles that float up so free,
They pop with a laugh, just me and the bee.
The stars peek out, it's a curious sight,
The moon's grinning down, what a delight!

In violet dreams, we'll dance and play,
Chasing the giggles till the break of day.
With every chuckle, the night feels right,
As we twirl beneath the soft starlight.

Petal-Soft Secrets

In a bloom of petals, secrets hide,
A ladybug whispers, 'Let's go for a ride!'
My stuffed bear nods with an earnest face,
It's time for adventures in the garden space.

We tiptoe past flowers, their scents so sweet,
Mimicking bees with a wiggly beat.
I twirl around like a dandelion's fluff,
But trip on a twig—oh, that's quite enough!

The breeze laughs gently, teasing my hair,
As I tell my bear about the cloud's flair.
We share our thoughts with a giggle and grin,
Nature's our stage, let the shenanigans begin!

With petals as soft as the tales we weave,
In this hilarious garden, we truly believe.
With each silly dance, and absurd little quest,
We treasure the moments and banter our best!

The Garden of Dreams

In the garden of dreams, where laughter grows,
A rabbit in slippers strikes a funny pose.
The daisies cheer in their white-frilled hats,
While frogs in bowties chat with the cats.

Under the trees, where shadows play hide,
A snail with a monocle strolls with pride.
He stops to debate with a wise old toad,
About the best way to carry a load.

The sun sets low, tickling each leaf,
I find a potato that's shaped like a chief.
With giggles and games, we dance all around,
In the garden of dreams, joy knows no bound.

So come join the fun, join the whimsical crew,
With flowers that giggle and skies painted blue.
In a world full of whimsy, the night starts to gleam,
Together we wander in the garden of dreams.

A Canvas of Dawn

The sun paints skies with orange and pink,
While squirrels dance around the kitchen sink.
Birds chirp loudly, giving fashion tips,
To a lazy cat with lazy hips.

The coffee brews, but spills on my shorts,
As I juggle breakfast like Olympic sports.
Pancakes flip, but always take a dive,
What a way to start the day alive!

With butter fingers, I toast my day,
A jammed-up toast chooses to betray.
Yet laughter spills like syrup on my plate,
In this morning chaos, my heart can't wait.

The Blush of Nostalgia

Once upon a time, I wore a bright hat,
Thought I was stunning, but I looked like a brat.
In family albums, I smile so wide,
Got frizzy hair; dad's plaid shirt as my guide.

The awkward dances at the school prom,
Two left feet, but I still brought the charm.
With neon colors and socks that don't match,
Every photo's a memory, a hilarious catch.

Now I giggle at those cringe-worthy styles,
Yet deep down inside, it all brings warm smiles.
Life's silly moments wrapped in a bow,
A laugh in every glance, a mirror to show.

Chasing Rose-Colored Dreams

In dreamy slumber, I chase candy skies,
With unicorns that wear sunglasses; what a surprise!
They tell me stories of cupcakes and fun,
But I wake up to broccoli, not glittery sun.

My pillow whispers secrets of mischief and glee,
While my dog snorts with laughter next to me.
The parakeet throws shade, acting all wise,
While I croak out tunes, a comical surprise.

Chasing dreams may lead to a jelly-filled mess,
But a life full of giggles? Oh, that's the best!
So let's frolic through fields with bubbles in hand,
In this wild, whimsical, candy-coated land.

Essence of Springtime

Flowers bloom, but so do my sneezes,
Allergies dance with the playful breezes.
Bees buzz around my head like a song,
I try to shoo them, but they're too strong.

The bunnies hop with their fluffy tails high,
While I trip over roots, oh my, oh my!
A picnic planned, but ants steal my fries,
They dine like kings; I only hear my cries.

Daisies tickle my feet, they want a parade,
But I'm busy sipping lemonade, homemade.
In this season laugh-fest, joy takes the spring,
Let's dance with the daisies and see what they bring!

Light Filtering Through Leaves

Sunlight dances on the ground,
Like a shy kid, not making a sound.
Leaves giggle softly as they sway,
Nature's light show, brightening the day.

A squirrel prances, tail held high,
He thinks he's the star, oh my, oh my!
With acorns as props, he strikes a pose,
While I try to capture his antics in prose.

Breezes play tag with the nearby grass,
Twirling like dancers, oh what a class!
I slip on a leaf, take a tumble down,
Laughter echoes, I'm the jester in town.

In this gleeful woodland, joy takes flight,
Every wrong step feels just so right.
Under the leaves, where the sunlight peeks,
Nature's humor is what everybody seeks.

Traces of Forgotten Gardens

Once there stood a flower so proud,
Now it's a memory, lost in the crowd.
Weeds in tuxedos roam about,
While gnats form a band, singing out loud.

Mud pies await the hands of a child,
Creating dessert, oh so wild!
A butterfly winks, painting the air,
As I trip on a root, unaware of my flair.

Bumbles buzz loudly, a curious bunch,
They think my picnic's a free lunch!
Dandelion wishes float through the scene,
Knocking my sandwich with a cheeky sheen.

In paths overgrown, hilarity brews,
Caught in a thicket, I can't find my shoes!
These gardens whisper tales of the past,
Where laughter and messiness forever last.

Embraces of Color

Colors burst forth, like a painter's spree,
Yellows and greens giggle, 'Look at me!'
Pinks poke fun at the dull greys nearby,
Even the violets wink with a sigh.

Sunflowers stand tall, making a fuss,
While daisies conspire without a bus.
Tulips lean in, sharing a joke,
As bumblebees buzz, all cloaked in smoke.

Rainbows sneak in with a cheeky smirk,
They tickle the clouds, do a little work.
One drop of paint here, a splash of delight,
Nature's own palette, oh, what a sight!

So here in the garden, with colors so bright,
Everything's giggling, what a funny sight.
Amidst hues and laughter that never gets old,
Each blossom a wit, or so I'm told.

Whispers of the Starlit Past

Stars twinkle mischief, playing peek-a-boo,
With dreams of long ago, shimmering through.
The moon throws a party, all shiny and round,
While old comets toast, drifting sound to sound.

Ghostly echoes of laughter drift past,
Stories of starlight, too wild to last.
The Milky Way chuckles, a cosmic delight,
As I fumble my way through the velvety night.

Meteor showers wiggle, in the dark, they groove,
While wishes go sailing, in cosmic move.
A space cat purrs, from afar, it seems,
Playing with shadows, of all my dreams.

Here in the void, with time slipping by,
Every twinkling wink makes me sigh.
With whispers of history flowing like wine,
Under starlit cover, it's all so fine.

Garden of Eternal Youth

In a garden where time stands still,
Grown-ups sip juice, it's quite the thrill.
With flip-flops on, they dance the day,
While squirrels cheer, hip-hip-hooray!

Sunflowers gossip, gossip they do,
Who wears what and who's dating who?
A fountain of laughter, bubbles so bright,
While ants do a conga, oh what a sight!

Vegetables giggle, they're all in a bunch,
Radishes hope for a salad crunch.
But carrots just chuckle, in soil tucked tight,
Wishing to join a garden delight!

So join our fun, take off your shoes,
In this youthful spot, there's nothing to lose.
With every giggle, we plant a seed,
In laughter's embrace, we're all freed!

Hues of Hope

In a world painted with colors so bright,
A purple cat purrs, oh what a sight!
Yellow elephants trot with great glee,
Sipping on lemonade, happy as can be.

Each shade whispers secrets, a tale to spin,
Of cakes made of clouds and a giraffe's win.
Orange birds sing of marshmallow skies,
While minty green frogs wear trendy ties.

Ribbons of rainbows twirl in the air,
As bubblegum butterflies dance without care.
They sprinkle the world with laughter and cheer,
Chasing away all the worries and fear.

So dip in the colors, swirl and create,
A canvas of fun that just can't wait.
With every hue, a giggle's released,
In this wacky world, joy never ceased!

The Petal Pathway

On a pathway of petals, soft underfoot,
Giggles emerge from a tiny sprout.
Ladybugs dance on a cobblestone track,
While mischief unfolds, there's no turning back!

Daisies wear sunglasses, cool as can be,
As bees throw a rave with buzzing harmony.
Butterflies flutter, on a donut-shaped breeze,
While grasshoppers strum their tiny cheese.

Lollipops whistle tunes to the sun,
While puddles reflect all the fun just begun.
Tickled by breezes that swirl all around,
The petals chuckle at the silliness found.

So skip down the pathway, and laugh out loud,
In this giggly garden, let joy be the crowd.
Each step is a melody, light and spry,
Beneath silly skies where dreams can't die!

Echoes of a Sunlit Past

In echoes of laughter, memories dance,
As shadows of socks do the silly prance.
A kite flies high, though it's tangled in trees,
Whispering tales with the faintest of breezes.

Silly faces carved in the pumpkin smile,
As spaghetti flops in a most graceful style.
The echoes of fun wrap around like a hug,
Reminding us all of that good ol' snug.

Ice cream dreams melt in the summer's glow,
While goofy goldfish swim to and fro.
In the corridors of laughter, we play,
For echoes of joy will never decay!

So gather your pals, don't be shy,
In the sunlit past, we'll always fly high.
With each shared story, we stitch together,
Echoes of fun that last forever!

Lush Hues of Memory

In the garden of laughter, we danced like fools,
With blooms tickling noses, breaking all rules.
Our pockets of sunshine, we'd toss in the air,
Chasing butterflies' giggles, without a care.

The daisies were whispering secrets so bright,
We'd twirl in their petals, a whimsical sight.
With honey-drenched dreams draped on our shoulders,
Each chuckle a rose that never grows older.

We'd sip on the nectar of mischief and glee,
Swapping stories that bloomed like wild raspberry tea.
The trees would all chuckle, their branches would sway,
As we painted the world in our own merry way.

Come revel in memories, both silly and sweet,
Where the laughter of ages and joyflowers meet.
In this vibrant tableau, we couldn't look back,
For the giggles of yesterday fill every track.

Dappled Light

Amidst the dappled shadows, we played hide and seek,
Wearing crowns of daisies, feeling oh so chic.
The sun's playful beams danced on our toes,
As giggles erupted and joy overflowed.

We strung up some laughter on branches so high,
As squirrels gave a nod, letting out a sigh.
The breeze snickered softly, tickling our skin,
In this zoo of delight, let the adventure begin!

We wore socks with sandals, which surely was bold,
But no one here cared, we were young, we were gold.
With puddles of puddles, we splashed through the cheer,
As our shadows did tumble, spilling joy far and near.

In this tapestry woven from sunlight and jest,
Where every wild moment felt like a fest.
We laughed at the clouds as they wandered on by,
Embracing the whims of a luminous sky.

The Enchanted Blossom

In a realm of odd petals, where giggles unwind,
Dandelions danced, leaving laughter behind.
With teacups of petals, we sipped on the breeze,
Sharing whispers of wonders among the tall trees.

The bees wore their tuxedos, buzzing with flair,
While ants put on shows, performing with care.
We traveled through hiccups, where silliness thrived,
Each blossom a tale where our joy was derived.

The moon got a chuckle, as shadows took flight,
Sketching silly stories in the soft, starry night.
With crickets composing our harmonious tune,
We sang silly ballads beneath the full moon.

A kingdom of giggles where silliness reigns,
In the garden of dreams, where humor sustains.
With friends at the forefront, the fun never stops,
As our hearts bloom like flowers in whimsical pops.

Flare of the Evening Sky

Underneath the twilight, where humor ignites,
We'd build castles of laughter, where silliness bites.
With fireflies lighting our paths, oh so bright,
Dancing shadows conspired to dim the night light.

We traded our worries for stars in a jar,
With wishes that giggled, our laughter the star.
The crickets all joined in, a concert of cheer,
As we shared silly secrets, each one loud and clear.

The moon took a selfie, gleefully wide,
While clouds wore their best, letting laughter decide.
Each flare in the sky held a story or two,
From the silliest moments, we laughed and we flew.

In this canvas of twilight, our joys intertwine,
With grins painted bright, like the sweetest red wine.
Underneath a vast sky where humor took flight,
We danced through the evening, hearts full of light.

Colorful Echoes

In gardens bright, I saw a bee,
He danced so wild, just like me!
With petals swirling, what a sight,
He stole my snack, oh, what a fright!

A parrot shouted, "Let's all play!"
I tried to join, but led astray.
With splashes of paint upon my shoes,
It seems I'm not the only one to lose!

A butterfly giggled in the sun,
Chasing the dancers, oh what fun!
But when I tripped, I laughed so loud,
I joined the ranks of the silly crowd!

In this wild splash of colors bright,
I'll paint my world from day to night.
With echoing laughs, I'll take my cue,
Bring on the fun, I'll color you!

The Petal Chronicles

In the park, a bloom took flight,
Waving at me, what a sight!
It said, "Join in, the fun is near!"
I tripped and fell, but had no fear.

A ladybug claimed to be the queen,
In shades of red, a royal scene.
She ruled the daisies with a smile,
While I performed a silly style!

The violets giggled, the sunbeam winked,
As I planned my dance, or so I think.
With twirls and spins, and quite a bump,
I joined the flowers in a happy jump!

These petals whisper stories sweet,
Of wobbly steps and dancing feet.
In this garden of whimsical tale,
I'll laugh and play and never pale!

Memories Caught in Bloom

A daisy bud boldly spoke to me,
"Let's host a party under the tree!"
With a shout, it called all the crew,
"Bring your snacks; it'll be a zoo!"

Amidst the scents of sweet delight,
I wore a crown that was far too tight.
The roses laughed, their petals wide,
As I stumbled forward, brimming with pride.

With confetti made of flower dust,
We danced in circles, as friends we trust.
But when I slipped on a berry pie,
The whole crew gasped, then laughed and cried!

So here's to blooms on sunny days,
With giggles echoing in sunlit rays.
In petals bright, we share our cheer,
Creating memories we hold so dear!

Tresses of Twilight

In the evening light, the flowers sway,
Whispering secrets at the end of day.
With tresses of twilight dancing free,
I joined the blooms, oh, what glee!

A clover, plucky, wore a hat,
Said, "Join the parade! What do you think of that?"
I marched along, my shoes askew,
As laughter rang from all my crew!

A sunflower winked, a beacon bright,
It guided us onward into the night.
With giggling petals twinkling fair,
We wove through meadows without a care.

In shadows cast by the moon's soft glow,
We danced in circles, putting on a show.
With the sweet scent of dusk in the air,
Our joyful antics, too funny to spare!

www.ingramcontent.com/pod-product-compliance
Lightning Source LLC
Chambersburg PA
CBHW071816160426
43209CB00003B/103